Let's Talk About
WHINING

Let's Talk About

WHINING

By JOY WILT BERRY

Illustrated by John Costanza
Edited by Orly Kelly
Designed by Jill Losson

GROLIER ENTERPRISES CORP.

Let's talk about WHINING.

Have you ever been around a person who has been whining for a long time?

When you are around a person who has been whining for a long time —

- how do you feel?
- what do you think?
- what do you do?

When you are around a person who is whining —

- you may be irritated and become upset;
- you may think that the person is not fun to be with;
- you may decide that you do not want to be around the person.

It is important to treat other people the way that you want to be treated.

If you do not want people to whine around you, you must not whine around them.

There are several reasons why you may whine. You may whine because *things aren't happening the way you want them to happen.* Maybe your parents have told you no, or they might have asked you to do something that you do not want to do. You may whine so that your parents will change their minds and let you have your own way.

But whining can only make things worse.

Don't whine when you do not get your way.
Do these things instead:

- Remember that you cannot have your
  own way all of the time. It is not good
  for you. It is not fair to the people
  around you.

- If you disagree with your parents,
  talk with them kindly. Give them
  some time to think about what you
  have said. What you say may cause
  them to change their minds. If it
  doesn't, don't talk about it anymore.
  If you keep talking, you will only
  frustrate yourself and make your
  parents angry.

You may whine because *you want attention.*
You may want your parents to notice you.
You may need to have them spend some time
with you.

But whining will not get you the kind of
attention you want or need.

Don't whine if you want attention. Do these things instead:

- Tell your parents kindly that you need some attention.
- If your parents are not able to give attention to you right away, set up a time when they can be with you.
  Then wait for that time to come, and do not bother your parents while you are waiting.

You may whine because *you are bored*. You may not have anything to do and you may think that whining will get your parents to entertain you.

But whining will not help you when you are bored. It will only make things worse.

Don't whine when you are bored. Do these things instead:

- Remember that *you* are responsible for keeping yourself busy. It is not up to anyone else to entertain you.

- Talk with your parents. Tell them politely that you are bored. Ask them to suggest things for you to do.

- If you do not like your parents' suggestions, come up with something to do on your own. Make sure that what you decide to do is all right with your parents.

You may whine because *you are hungry, tired, or sick*. When your body needs something or when it is not feeling well, you may become cranky.

You may want to whine.

When this happens, you must take care of your body.

- Eat some nutritious food if you are hungry.
- Get some rest if you are tired.
- Do what the doctor and your parents tell you to do when you are sick.

You may whine because *it is a habit*.

A habit is something you do so often or for so long that you do it without thinking. When whining becomes a habit, you will whine often without realizing what you are doing.

To break the habit of whining, ask the people around you to help you. Have them tell you when you are whining. Whenever they tell you that you are whining, stop it immediately. Do this until you do not whine anymore.

When you whine, your parents may need to do one of two things:

- Your parents may need to *ignore you* when you whine. If they ignore you, it does not mean that they do not love you. They may ignore you because they want you to learn that whining is not a good way for you to get attention.

- Your parents may need to *get away from you* when you whine. If they walk away or send you away, it does not mean that they do not love you. It is what your parents may need to do so that your whining will not upset them or the other people around you.

If you want to be happy, you will treat other people the way you want to be treated.

This means that you will not whine around others, because you do not want them to whine around you.